DECIMALS
Addition & Subtraction

Allan D. Suter

McGraw Hill **Contemporary**

Series Editor: Mitch Rosin
Executive Editor: Linda Kwil
Production Manager: Genevieve Kelley
Marketing Manager: Sean Klunder
Cover Design: Steve Strauss, ¡Think! Design

 **Contemporary**

Send all inquiries to:
McGraw-Hill/Contemporary
130 East Randolph Street, Suite 400
Chicago, Illinois 60601

ISBN: 0-07-287106-7

Printed in the United States of America.

1 2 3 4 5 6 7 8 9 10 QPD/QPD 08 07 06 05 04 03

The McGraw·Hill Companies

■ Contents

1. In the number 9.472, which digit is in the tenths place?

    Answer: _____

2. Use numbers to write eight and thirty-six hundredths.

    Answer: _____

3. Which of the following decimals has the same value as .42:
   .042, .0042, .420, or 4.2?

    Answer: _____

4. Which of the following decimals has the greatest value:
   2.055, 2.5, or 2.499?

    Answer: _____

5. 18 + 3.27 =

    Answer: _____

6.   29.2
         7.76
       + 3.87

    Answer: _____

7. 7.22 + 93.61 + 5.27 =

    Answer: _____

8. 17.2 + 9.74 + 3 =

    Answer: _____

9. 192.3 + 3.01 + 91.19 =

    Answer: _____

10.   19.06
       − 5.39

    Answer: _____

11. $4.3 - 4.08 =$

Answer: _____

12. $43 - 9.36 =$

Answer: _____

13. $21.3 - 3.56 =$

Answer: _____

14. $41 - 18.65 =$

Answer: _____

15. Luis had $20.00. If he spent $12.53, how much money did he have left?

Answer: _____

16. Ken has $14.35 more than Mary. Mary has $9.35. How much money does Ken have?

Answer: _____

17. The distance from Jefferson to Beacon is 49.6 miles. The distance from Beacon to Mayville is 36.7 miles. What is the total distance from Jefferson to Mayville by way of Beacon?

Answer: _____

18. Susan's normal temperature is 98.6°. When sick, Susan's temperature reached 103°. How much above normal was her temperature when she had a fever?

Answer: _____

19. A plumber welded a pipe that was 11.5 inches long onto another piece of pipe that was 8.75 inches long. What was the length of the joined pieces?

Answer: _____

20. The town of Jefferson wants to raise $1.2 million for a new sports center. So far they have raised $.88 million. How much more money do they need?

Answer: _____

Evaluation Chart

On the following chart, circle the number of any problem you missed. The column after the problem number tells you the pages where those problems are taught. Based on your score, your teacher may ask you to study specific sections of this book. However, to thoroughly review your skills, begin with Unit 1 on page 7.

Skill Area	Pretest Problem Number	Skill Section	Review Page
Place Value	1, 2, 3, 4	7–24	25
Addition	5, 6, 7, 8, 9	26–34	35
Subtraction	10, 11, 12, 13, 14	45–55	56
Addition Word Problems	16, 17, 19	36–43	44
Subtraction Word Problems	15, 18, 20	57–66	67
Life-Skills Math	All	68–73	74

Meaning of Tenths

Four tenths (.4) are shaded

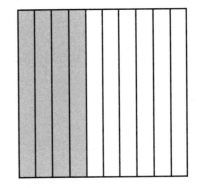

Tenths—a one-place decimal

The square on the right has been divided into 10 equal parts. Each part is one tenth of the square. Four tenths can be written as a decimal (.4) to show 4 out of 10.

4 out of 10

.4

1. Shade 6 tenths.

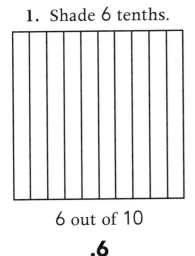

6 out of 10

.6

2. Shade 9 tenths.

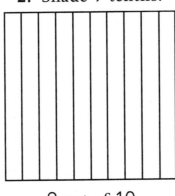

9 out of 10

.9

3. Shade 1 tenth.

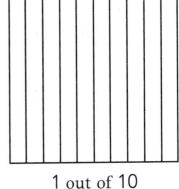

1 out of 10

.1

The number line below is divided into ten equal parts.

4. Connect the boxes to the line.

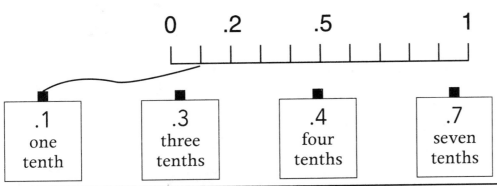

Comparing Tenths

The number line below is divided into ten equal parts.

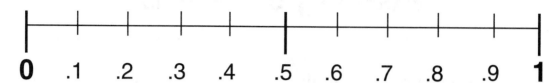

You compare decimals the same way you compare whole numbers.

Compare .7 and .5

Think: 7 is greater than 5, so **.7 is greater than .5**

Compare the decimals.

1. Eight tenths (.8) is _____ than five tenths (.5).
   _{greater or less}

2. One tenth (.1) is _____ than two tenths (.2).
   _{greater or less}

3. Two tenths (.2) is _____ than eight tenths (.8).
   _{greater or less}

4. Four tenths (.4) is _____ than nine tenths (.9).
   _{greater or less}

5. Five tenths (.5) is _____ than three tenths (.3).
   _{greater or less}

6. Eight tenths (.8) is _____ than one tenth (.1).
   _{greater or less}

7. Five tenths (.5) is _____ than two tenths (.2).
   _{greater or less}

8. Seven tenths (.7) is _____ than two tenths (.2).
   _{greater or less}

9. Moving to the left on the number line, numbers get _____ .
   _{larger or smaller}

10. Moving to the right on the number line, numbers get _____ .
    _{larger or smaller}

Meaning of Hundredths

Hundredths—a two-place decimal

Each square is divided into one hundred (100) equal parts.

1. Shade .35

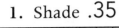
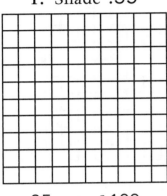

35 out of 100

2. Shade .81

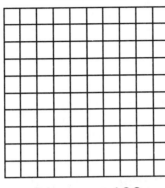

81 out of 100

3. Shade .09

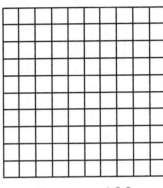

9 out of 100

35 out of 100 is .35 (thirty-five hundredths).

81 out of 100 is .81 (eighty-one hundredths).

9 out of 100 is .09 (nine hundredths).

↑ zero puts 9 in the hundredths place

Show how decimals are used in money.

4. 1 dollar is equal to __100__ pennies.

5. 15 pennies are equal to fifteen hundredths (._1_ _5_) of one dollar.
   _{decimal}

6. 75 pennies are equal to seventy-five hundredths (.____ ____) of one dollar.
   _{decimal}

7. 25 pennies are equal to twenty-five hundredths (.____ ____) of one dollar.
   _{decimal}

8. 1 penny is equal to one hundredth (._0_ ____) of one dollar.
   _{decimal}

9. 50 pennies are equal to fifty hundredths (.____ ____) of one dollar.
   _{decimal}

10. 4 pennies are equal to four hundredths (._0_ ____) of one dollar.
    _{decimal}

Comparing Hundredths

Each square is divided into 100 equal parts.

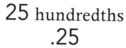

25 hundredths
.25

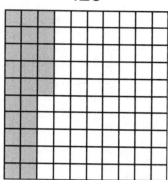

75 hundredths
.75

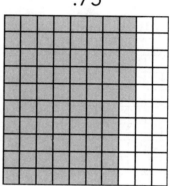

You compare decimals the same way you compare whole numbers.

Compare .25 and .75

Think: 25 is less than 75, so **.25 is less than .75**

Compare the decimals.

1. 15 hundredths (.15) is _____ than 5 hundredths (.05).
   _{greater or less}

2. 8 hundredths (.08) is _____ than 4 hundredths (.04).
   greater or less

3. 65 hundredths (.65) is _____ than 35 hundredths (.35).
   greater or less

4. 28 hundredths (.28) is _____ than 92 hundredths (.92).
   greater or less

5. 1 hundredth (.01) is _____ than 5 hundredths (.05).
   greater or less

6. 85 hundredths (.85) is _____ than 58 hundredths (.58).
   greater or less

7. 3 hundredths (.03) is _____ than 9 hundredths. (.09).
   greater or less

8. 28 hundredths (.28) is _____ than 41 hundredths (.41).
   greater or less

Meaning of Thousandths

Thousandths—a three-place decimal

Write the decimals.

Decimal

1. 35 thousandths means 35 out of 1,000.

. 0 3 5

Write a zero so last digit is in thousandths place.

2. 69 thousandths means 69 out of 1,000.

. 0 __ __

3. 350 thousandths means 350 out of 1,000.

. 3 __ __

4. 936 thousandths means 936 out of 1,000.

. __ __ __

5. 525 thousandths means 525 out of 1,000.

. __ __ __

6. 250 thousandths means _____ out of 1,000.

. 2 5 0

7. 40 thousandths means _____ out of_____.

. 0 __ __

8. 485 thousandths means _____ out of _____.

. __ __ __

9. 806 thousandths means _____ out of _____.

. __ __ __

10. 15 thousandths means _____ out of _____.

. 0 __ __

11. 685 thousandths means _____ out of _____.

. __ __ __

12. 167 thousandths means _____ out of _____.

. __ __ __

Comparing Thousandths

You compare decimals the same way you compare whole numbers.

Compare .856 and .305

Think: 856 is greater than 305, so **.856 is greater than .305**

Compare the decimals.

1. .304 is _____ than .403
   greater or less

2. .723 is _____ than .722
   greater or less

3. .208 is _____ than .108
   greater or less

4. .405 is _____ than .504
   greater or less

5. .900 is _____ than .889
   greater or less

6. .008 is _____ than .005
   greater or less

7. .345 is _____ than .358
   greater or less

8. .110 is _____ than .101
   greater or less

9. .075 is _____ than .057
   greater or less

10. .002 is _____ than .012
    greater or less

Place-Value Readiness

Fill in the place-value chart from the list below.

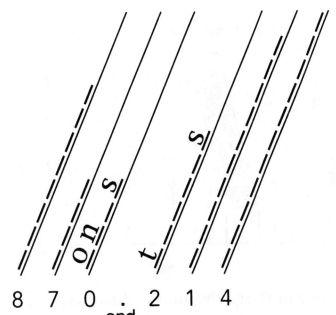

LIST
hundreds
tens
thousandths
tenths
hundredths
ones

A. 8 7 0 . 2 1 4
              and

Eight hundred seventy **and** two hundred fourteen thousandths

Use 67.452 for problems 1–5.

1. The 7 has what place value? _____

2. The 5 has what place value? _____

3. The 4 has what place value? _____

4. The 2 has what place value? _____

5. The 6 has what place value? _____

Use 81.072 for problems 6–10.

6. What digit is in the tenths place? _____

7. What digit is in the tens place? _____

8. What digit is in the hundredths place? _____

9. What digit is in the ones place? _____

10. What digit is in the thousandths place? _____

Place Values

Fill in the correct digits for each place-value position.

1. Seventy-one and six tenths has

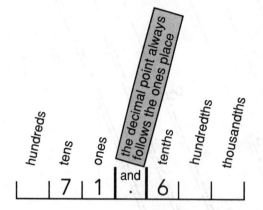

   a) _____ tens

   b) _____ one

   c) _____ tenths

2. Ninety-four and thirty-five hundredths has

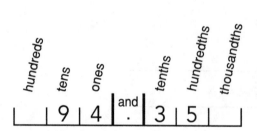

   a) _____ tens

   b) _____ ones

   c) _____ tenths

   d) _____ hundredths

3. Eighty-nine and four hundred sixty-three thousandths has

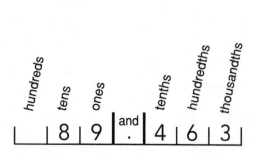

   a) _____ tens

   b) _____ ones

   c) _____ tenths

   d) _____ hundredths

   e) _____ thousandths

Reading Decimals

A place-value chart will help you read and write decimals.

The decimal point is read as "and."

↓

71.647

71 and **647** thousandths

Fill in the place-value chart.

	tens	ones	and	tenths	hundredths	thousandths	
1. 71.647	7	1	.	6	4	7	_71_ and _647_ thousandths
2. 50.94							_____ and _____ hundredths
3. 1.6							_____ and _____ tenths
4. 16.345							_____ and _____ thousandths
5. 3.7							_____ and _____ tenths
6. 8.04							_____ and _____ hundredths
7. 17.39							_____ and _____ hundredths
8. 98.507							_____ and _____ thousandths
9. 7.53							_____ and _____ hundredths
10. 84.2							_____ and _____ tenths
11. 4.008							_____ and _____ thousandths
12. 7.45							_____ and _____ hundredths
13. 6.19							_____ and _____ hundredths
14. 29.133							_____ and _____ thousandths
15. 2.4							_____ and _____ tenths

Write the Place Value

Use words from the list to fill in the place values.

4.9

1. The 4 is in the _____ones_____ place.

2. The 9 is in the _____ place.

4.15

3. The 5 is in the _____ place.

4. The 1 is in the _____ place.

5. The 4 is in the _____ place.

102.35

6. The 5 is in the _____ place.

7. The 0 is in the _____ place.

8. The 3 is in the _____ place.

9. The 1 is in the _____ place.

96.257

10. The 2 is in the _____ place.

11. The 5 is in the _____ place.

12. The 9 is in the _____ place.

13. The 7 is in the _____ place.

628.943

14. The 6 is in the _____ place.

15. The 9 is in the _____ place.

16. The 3 is in the _____ place.

17. The 4 is in the _____ place.

18. The 2 is in the _____ place.

LIST

ones

hundredths

tens

thousandths

hundreds

tenths

Identify the Digit

Draw a circle around your answer.

1. Which of these decimal numbers has a 5 in the hundredths place?

    461.065   513.521   100.545   927.452

2. Which of these decimal numbers has a 3 in the tenths place?

    84.23   469.36   37.54   63.91

3. Which of these decimal numbers has a 7 in the thousandths place?

    6,431.730   7,419.109   2,314.067   4,732.471

Build the decimal numbers.

4. 9 in the tenths place
   4 in the hundredths place

   .__9__ __4__

5. 8 in the tenths place
   7 in the ones place
   9 in the tens place

   ___ ___ . ___

6. 6 in the thousandths place
   0 in the tenths place
   5 in the hundredths place

   . ___ ___ ___

7. 0 in the tenths place
   1 in the tens place
   5 in the ones place
   4 in the hundredths place

   ___ ___ . ___ ___

8. 8 in the thousandths place
   4 in the tenths place
   5 in the hundredths place

   . ___ ___ ___

9. 1 in the ones place
   5 in the hundredths place
   4 in the tenths place
   3 in the hundreds place
   2 in the tens place

   ___ ___ ___ . ___ ___

10. 4 in the tenths place
    3 in the tens place
    5 in the hundreds place
    2 in the ones place
    7 in the thousandths place
    9 in the hundredths place

    ___ ___ ___ . ___ ___ ___

Zeros in Decimals

Zeros may or may not change the value of a decimal.

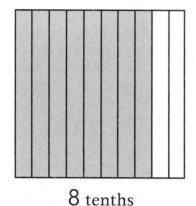

8 tenths

.8   is the same as   .80

80 hundredths

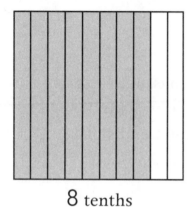

8 tenths

.8   is **not** the same as .08

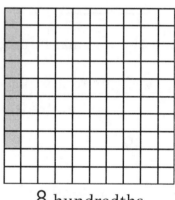

8 hundredths

Adding a zero **to the end** of a decimal changes its form, but not its value.

.8 = .80 = .800

Adding a zero **to the front** of a decimal changes its form **and** its value.

.8 is **not** the same as .08 or .008

In each row, circle the decimals that have the same value as the first number.

1. **.23**	(.230)	2.30	.0023	(.2300)
2. **.046**	.0046	.460	.0460	.046
3. **.1**	.01	.10	.100	1.0
4. **3.5**	3.50	3.05	3.500	3.050
5. **.07**	.7	.070	.007	.07
6. **9.08**	9.080	9.8	9.80	9.08

Writing Zeros to Hold Place Values

These numbers are **not** the same:

.7	.07	.007
7 tenths	7 hundredths	7 thousandths

Use zeros to "hold" numbers in the correct place value.

___

Write the decimal forms of the numbers.

1. 37 thousandths   . _0_ ___ ___   The 7 is in the thousandths place.

2. 6 hundredths   . ___ ___   The 6 is in the hundredths place.

3. 9 tenths   . ___

4. 16 hundredths   . ___ ___

5. 427 thousandths   . ___ ___ ___

6. 1 thousandth   . ___ ___ ___

7. 1 and 14 thousandths ___ . ___ ___ ___   Write a decimal point for "and."

8. 16 and 9 hundredths   ___ ___ . ___ ___

9. 427 and 3 tenths   ___ ___ ___ . ___

10. 7 and 7 thousandths ___ . ___ ___ ___

11. 5 hundredths   . ___ ___

12. 3 tenths   . ___

Words to Decimals

Complete the place-value chart.

	hundreds	tens	ones	and	tenths	hundredths	thousandths
1. Six and four tenths			6	.	4		
2. Fifteen and six hundredths				.			
3. Three hundred forty-five thousandths							
4. One hundred and twenty-one hundredths							
5. Eight hundred ninety-four and six tenths							
6. Seven thousandths							
7. Ninety-three and fifty-four thousandths							
8. Seven and four tenths							
9. Two hundred seven and seventy-one hundredths							
10. Three thousandths							
11. Five hundred thirty-nine thousandths							
12. Nine hundred forty-five and three hundredths							
13. Three and eight thousandths							
14. Eight tenths							
15. One hundred five and one hundredth							

Find the Number

Match the letters and the numbers.

__d__	1. Nine and thirty-two hundredths	a) 9.032
_____	2. Nine hundred thirty-two	b) 932
_____	3. Nine and thirty-two thousandths	c) 93.2
_____	4. Ninety-three and two tenths	d) 9.32
_____	5. Five hundred forty-eight	a) 5.048
_____	6. Five and forty-eight hundredths	b) 5.48
_____	7. Five and forty-eight thousandths	c) 548
_____	8. Fifty-four and eight tenths	d) 54.8
_____	9. Seventy and sixteen hundredths	a) 701.6
_____	10. Seven and sixteen thousandths	b) 7,016
_____	11. Seven hundred one and six tenths	c) 70.16
_____	12. Seven thousand sixteen	d) 7.016
_____	13. Three and eight tenths	a) 3.08
_____	14. Three and eight thousandths	b) 3.8
_____	15. Thirty-eight	c) 3.008
_____	16. Three and eight hundredths	d) 38
_____	17. Six and four hundred seventy-two thousandths	a) 6,472
_____	18. Six hundred forty-seven and two tenths	b) 6.472
_____	19. Sixty-four and seventy-two hundredths	c) 647.2
_____	20. Six thousand, four hundred seventy-two	d) 64.72

Expanding Decimals

Complete the expanded forms.

1. $.73 = . \underline{}_{\text{tenths}} + . \underline{} 0 \underline{}_{\text{hundredths}}$

2. $.984 = . \underline{}_{\text{tenths}} + . \underline{}\,\underline{}_{\text{hundredths}} + . \underline{}\,\underline{}\,\underline{}_{\text{thousandths}}$

3. $8.275 = 8 + . \underline{} + . \underline{}\,\underline{} + . \underline{}\,\underline{}\,\underline{}$

4. $.761 = . \underline{} + . \underline{}\,\underline{} + . \underline{}\,\underline{}\,\underline{}$

5. $75.94 = 70 + \underline{} + . \underline{} + . \underline{}\,\underline{}$

6. $5.693 = \underline{} + . \underline{} + . \underline{}\,\underline{} + . \underline{}\,\underline{}\,\underline{}$

7. $.94 = . \underline{} + . \underline{}\,\underline{}$

8. $4.386 = \underline{} + . \underline{} + . \underline{}\,\underline{} + . \underline{}\,\underline{}\,\underline{}$

Comparing Decimals

Adding a zero after the last digit of a decimal does not change its value.

.5 = .50

.5   =   .50

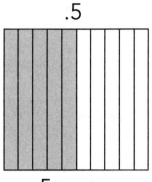 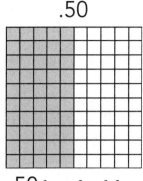

5 tenths   =   50 hundredths

Sometimes decimals do not have the same number of digits. To help you compare, you can add zeros so the decimals have the same number of decimal places. You compare decimals the same way you compare whole numbers.

Compare .8 and .59

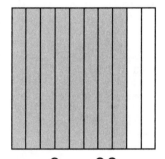 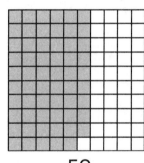

.8 or .80   .59

STEP 1	STEP 2	STEP 3
Add a zero to .8 and compare. .8 = .80 .59 = .59	Compare as whole numbers. 80 59	Think: 80 is greater than 59, so .8 is greater than .59.

Use the symbols < (less than), > (greater than), or = (equal to) to complete the problems below.

1. .8 is _____ .79
   <, >, or =

2. .4 is _____ .44
   <, >, or =

3. .3 is _____ .30
   <, >, or =

4. .5 is _____ .38
   <, >, or =

5. .08 is _____ .18
   <, >, or =

6. .107 is _____ .2
   <, >, or =

Ordering Decimals

You may need to put several decimals in order. Add as many zeros as you need to give the decimals the same number of places.

Write in order from **least** to **greatest**: 2.3, 2.37, and 2.346

<table>
<tr><td colspan="3" align="center">STEP 1</td><td colspan="2" align="center">STEP 2</td></tr>
<tr><td colspan="3" align="center">Write zeros so the decimals have the same number of places.</td><td colspan="2" align="center">Compare as whole numbers.</td></tr>
<tr><td>2.3</td><td>=</td><td>2.300</td><td>2,300</td><td>1. least</td></tr>
<tr><td>2.37</td><td>=</td><td>2.370</td><td>2,370</td><td>3. greatest</td></tr>
<tr><td>2.346</td><td>=</td><td>2.346</td><td>2,346</td><td>2. middle</td></tr>
</table>

The order from **least** to **greatest** is: 2.3, 2.346, 2.37

Follow the above steps and then write the decimals in order from **least** to **greatest**.

1. 4.2   4.279   4.25

    _____ _____ _____
    least   greatest

2. 5.841   5.03   4.25

    _____ _____ _____
    least   greatest

3. 7.01   7.4   7.032

    _____ _____ _____
    least   greatest

4. 17.8   15.98   15.981

    _____ _____ _____
    least   greatest

5. 94.3   94.301   94.3

    _____ _____ _____
    least   greatest

6. 13.05   13.5   13.58

    _____ _____ _____
    least   greatest

7. 5.30   3.50   3.05

    _____ _____ _____
    least   greatest

8. .378   3.49   3.5

    _____ _____ _____
    least   greatest

Decimal Place-Value Review

Answer the following problem.

1. .467 is _____ than .407

greater or less

Write the decimals in order from least to greatest.

6.   3.75   .375   37.5

   _____   _____   _____
   least   greatest

Use 54.982 for problems 2–5.

2. The 5 has what place value?

   _____

3. The 9 has what place value?

   _____

4. The 2 has what place value?

   _____

5. The 8 has what place value?

   _____

Write the numbers for problems 7–9.

7. Ninety-three and two tenths

8. Nine hundred thirty-two

9. Nine and thirty-two thousandths

Use <, >, = to complete the problem.

10. .38 _____ .09

Steps for Addition

Step 1: Line up the decimal points and place values.

Step 2: Bring down the decimal point for the answer.

Step 3: Add the numbers. You can regroup over the decimal point.

$5.4 + 1.3 =$

```
        line up
    ↓   decimal
  5.4   points
+ 1.3
─────
  6.7   bring down
     ↑  the decimal
        point
```

A. $3.6 + 2.5 =$

```
              regroup
(1) ←──────── to the
  3.6         ones
+ 2.5         place
─────
__ . __
 finish
```

B. $8.5 + 3.7 =$

```
         (1)
  8.5
+ 3.7
─────
___ . __
 finish
```

Line up the decimal points and place values. Add the numbers.

1. $3.2 + 4.5 =$

```
  3.2
+ 4.5
─────
__ . __
 finish
```

4. $9.3 + 3.9 =$

7. $7.6 + 3.7 =$

2. $5.1 + 5.4 =$

5. $6.5 + 8.6 =$

8. $5.5 + 6.8 =$

3. $2.5 + 3.2 =$

6. $2.4 + 5.9 =$

9. $7.4 + 3.6 =$

Adding Tenths, Hundredths, and Thousandths

Step 1: Line up the decimal points and place values.

Step 2: Bring down the decimal point for the answer.

Step 3: Add the numbers. Regroup when necessary.

.6 + .9 =

think zeros →
$$\begin{array}{r} 0.6 \\ +0.9 \\ \hline 1.5 \end{array}$$

A. .74 + .32 =

( )
$$\begin{array}{r} 0.74 \\ + 0.32 \\ \hline \_\_.\_\_\_ \end{array}$$
finish

B. .845 + .653 =

( )
$$\begin{array}{r} 0.845 \\ + 0.653 \\ \hline \_\_.\_\_\_\_ \end{array}$$
finish

Add the numbers. Regroup when necessary.

1. .5 + .6 =

( )
$$\begin{array}{r} 0.5 \\ + 0.6 \\ \hline \_\_.\_\_ \end{array}$$
finish

2. .3 + .7 =

3. .4 + .8 =

4. .97 + .64 =

5. .59 + .28 =

6. .06 + .05 =

7. .930 + .132 =

8. .485 + .017 =

9. .739 + .887 =

Adding Mixed Decimals

Mixed decimals combine whole numbers and decimals.

Step 1: Line up the decimal points and place values.

Step 2: Bring down the decimal point for the answer.

Step 3: Add the numbers. Regroup when necessary.

$8.64 + 5.42 =$ **A.** $9.67 + 5.94 =$ **B.** $7.03 + 9.25 =$

```
(1)            line up
 8.64          decimal
+5.42          points
------
14.06
```

```
( )( )
 9.67
+5.94
------
__.__
 finish
```

```
 7.03
+9.25
------
__.__
 finish
```

Add the numbers. Regroup if necessary.

1. $3.97 + 8.37 =$
```
( )( )
 3.97
+8.37
------
__.__
 finish
```

4. $6.41 + 5.20 =$

7. $4.13 + 2.24 =$

2. $7.01 + 3.08 =$

5. $5.09 + 3.46 =$

8. $1.80 + 4.91 =$

3. $3.97 + 8.03 =$

6. $5.94 + 7.67 =$

9. $9.58 + 6.95 =$

Think Zero

Step 1: Line up the decimal points and place values.

Step 2: Bring down the decimal point for the answer.

Step 3: Add the decimals and whole numbers.
"Think Zero" where there is an empty space.

$28.5 + 6.8 =$ A. $47.8 + 2.3 =$ B. $397.2 + 85.4 =$

```
think  (1)(1)
zero ↘ 2 8 . 5
     + 0 6 . 8
     ─────────
       3 5 . 3
```

```
   ( )( )
   4 7 . 8
 +   2 . 3
 ─────────
 ___ . __
  finish
```

```
   ( )( )
 3 9 7 . 2
 + 8 5 . 4
 ─────────
 ____ . __
   finish
```

Add the numbers. Write in zeros when necessary.

1. $97.8 + 3.2 =$
```
   ( )( )
   9 7 . 8
 +   3 . 2
 ─────────
 ___ . __
  finish
```

4. $57.8 + 9.2 =$

7. $889.4 + 16.3 =$

2. $15.2 + 1.9 =$ 5. $36.2 + 3.7 =$ 8. $486.4 + 57.2 =$

3. $45.6 + 1.9 =$ 6. $48.6 + 1.3 =$ 9. $38.2 + 3.5 =$

Zeros as Placeholders

When you add decimals, you line up the decimal points. Sometimes that leaves an "empty" place at the **end** of a number. Write in a zero to fill in that place.

Remember: adding one or more zeros at the end of a decimal does not change its value.

A. 5.48 + 9.8 =
( )
```
    5.48
  + 9.80  ←  write in zero
  ——.——
    finish
```

B. 34.6 + 9.47 =
( )( )
```
   34.60
  + 9.47
  ——.——
   finish
```

C. 4.932 + 1.4 =
( )( )
```
   4.932
  +1.400
  ——.——
   finish
```

Add the mixed decimals. Write in zero as a placeholder when necessary.

1. 7.45 + 2.9 =
( )
```
   7.45
  +2.90
  ——.——
   finish
```

4. 26.8 + 6.25 =

7. 3.774 + 9.3 =

2. 4.63 + 5.7 =

5. 69.3 + 2.58 =

8. 34.019 + 6.4 =

3. 38.76 + 5.4 =

6. 1.4 + 5.36 =

9. 7.883 + 2.7 =

Writing Decimal Points

When you add decimals, you may need to write a decimal point to the right of whole numbers.

6 = 6.   A. 61 = _____ _____ .↖   C. 144 = _____ _____ _____↖

18 = 18.   B. 522 = _____ _____ _____↖ D.   2 = _____↖

You write a decimal point and zeros when you add a whole number and a mixed decimal.

Add 7.98 + 6.

$$\begin{array}{r} 7.98 \\ +\ 6.00 \\ \hline 13.98 \end{array}$$

What is 430 + 7.92?

$$\begin{array}{r} 430.00 \\ +\ \ \ \ 7.92 \\ \hline 437.92 \end{array}$$

Add the whole numbers and mixed decimals. Write a decimal point and zeros where necessary.

1. 5.38 + 6 =

$$\begin{array}{r} 5.38 \\ +\ 6.00 \\ \hline \end{array}$$
___ ___ . ___
finish

3. 13.9 + 20 =

$$\begin{array}{r} 13.9 \\ +\ 20.0 \\ \hline \end{array}$$
___ ___ . ___
finish

5. 19 + 3.75 =

2. 18 + 6.93 =

$$\begin{array}{r} 18.00 \\ +\ 6.93 \\ \hline \end{array}$$
___ ___ . ___
finish

4. 5.16 + 4 =

6. 9.63 + 7 =

Write Zeros When Necessary

When you add decimals, write zeros to have the same number of decimal places.

$63 + 17.8 =$

whole number ↱

$47.6 + 338.72 =$

↰ two decimal places

A.
$$63.0$$
$$+ 17.8$$
—— . —
finish

B.
$$47.60$$
$$+ 338.72$$
——— . ——
finish

Add the numbers. Use zeros to fill in place values when necessary.

1. $5.2 + 4.7 =$

4. $16 + 1.94 =$

7. $6.91 + 8 =$

2. $15.2 + 4.79 =$

5. $4.56 + 3 =$

8. $15 + 4.7 =$

3. $9.401 + 18 =$

6. $7.93 + 25 =$

9. $10.45 + 5.65 =$

Lining Up Decimals

Practice lining up the numbers below.

$$13.04 + 8 + 2.1 + .79 = \begin{array}{r} 1\underline{3}.\underline{04} \\ \underline{8}.\underline{00} \\ \underline{2}.\underline{10} \\ .\underline{79} \end{array}$$

Write in zeros to get the same number of decimal places.

Copy the decimal numbers. Line them up to the right and the left of the decimal point. **Do not work the problems.**

1. $613.049 + .62 + .953 + .9 =$

    $$\begin{array}{r} \_\_\_.\_\_\_ \\ .\_\_0 \\ .\_\_\_ \\ + \quad .\_00 \\ \hline \end{array}$$

4. $\$21.40 + \$5.07 + \$51 =$

2. $2.95 + 62 + 45.39 + 3.846 =$

    $$\begin{array}{r} \_.\_\_0 \\ \_\_.000 \\ \_\_.390 \\ + \quad 3.846 \\ \hline \end{array}$$

5. $5.46 + 93.7 + 2.467 + 45.06 =$

3. $312.749 + 51.09 + 2.6 =$

6. $3.2 + .985 + .46 + 9 =$

Practice Helps

Line up the numbers and add. Write in zeros where necessary.

1. 7.49 + .053 + 21 =

$$\begin{array}{r} 7.490 \\ .053 \\ + \ 21.000 \\ \hline \\ \underline{\quad}.\underline{\quad\quad} \\ \text{finish} \end{array}$$

5. 2.95 + 3.46 + .45 =

2. 4.53 + 5 + 9.34 =

6. 36 + 1.4 + 45.13 =

3. 14.8 + .4 + .326 =

7. .129 + .32 + 9.4 =

4. 1.96 + 3.69 + .95 =

8. .9 + 36.9 + 84.07 =

Addition Review

1. Circle the decimal that has the **same value** as the first number.

   2.04   2.004   2.040   .204

2. Write the decimal form of the number.

   18 and 32 thousandths

3. Compare the decimals.

   .203 is _____ .3

$<, >,$ or $=$

4. Order the decimals from **least** to **greatest**.

   7.15   7.05   7.105

For problems 5–12, practice your addition skills.

5. $.132 + .417 =$

6. $.9 + .4 =$

7. $2.625 + 3.603 =$

8. $1.37 + 1.4 =$

9. $46.645 + 15.712 =$

10. $8.634 + 1.7 =$

11. $.531 + 2.62 + .08 =$

12. $17 + .046 =$

Decimals and Money

Our money system is based on decimals.

penny

1 cent = 1¢
.01 dollar = $.01

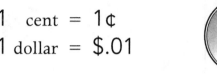
quarter

25 cents = 25¢
.25 dollar = $.25

nickel

5 cents = 5¢
.05 dollar = $.05

half-dollar

50 cents = 50¢
.50 dollar = $.50

dime

10 cents = 10¢
.10 dollar = $.10

dollar bill

100 cents = 100¢
1 dollar = $1.00

Match each coin with its value in decimal form.

_____ 1. penny   a. $.50

_____ 2. nickel   b. $.05

_____ 3. dime   c. $.01

_____ 4. quarter   d. $.25

_____ 5. half-dollar   e. $1.00

_____ 6. dollar   f. $.10

Working with Money

There are times when you will need to write money amounts in decimal form.

= $1 + .25 + .01 + .01 = $1.27
<u>answer</u>

= .10 + .10 + .25 + .01 = $.46
<u>answer</u>

Write each amount in decimal form using dollars and cents.

1. = ____ + ____ + ____ + ____ + ____ =

$_____
answer

2. = ____ + ____ + ____ + ____ + ____ =

$_____
answer

3. = ____ + ____ + ____ + ____ + ____ =

$_____
answer

4. = ____ + ____ + ____ + ____ + ____ =

$_____
answer

Writing Number Sentences

A number sentence can help you organize information and solve problems.

Write a number sentence to solve each problem.

1. $7.45 added to $3.15 is how much money?

_____ __+__ _____ = $___.___
number · operation symbol · number · answer

The total amount of money is $_____.

2. $13.05 and $5.62 total how many dollars?

_____ _____ _____ = $___.___
number · operation symbol · number · answer

The total amount of money is $_____.

3. $75.11 increased by $9.28 is how much money?

_____ _____ _____ = $___.___
number · operation symbol · number · answer

$75.11 increased by $9.28 is $_____.

4. $45.00 and $7.99 together equal how many dollars and cents?

_____ _____ _____ = $___.___
number · operation symbol · number · answer

$45.00 and $7.99 together equal $_____.

5. Combine $.68 and $6.45.

_____ _____ _____ = $__.___
number · operation symbol · number · answer

$.68 and $6.45 combined is $_____.

6. Find the sum of $9.98 and $15.00.

_____ _____ _____ = $___.___
number · operation symbol · number · answer

The sum of $9.98 and $15.00 is $_____.

Number Sentences

1. Read over the facts several times to make sure you understand them.

2. Think about the facts in the problem and what you are being asked to find.

3. Complete the number sentence for each problem.

4. Ask yourself, "Does the answer make sense?"

Complete a number sentence for each problem. Label your answers.

1. Maria stopped at a couple of stores on her way home from work. She spent $17.35 at one store and $6.92 at another. How much did Maria spend in all?

_____ _____ _____ = _____
number operation number   answer
        symbol

4. Bruce earned $25.50 and Sue earned $19.75. How much are their combined earnings?

_____ _____ _____ = _____
number operation number   answer
        symbol

2. The price of dinner was $15.92 plus $1.32 tax. What was the total for dinner including tax?

_____ _____ _____ = _____
number operation number   answer
        symbol

5. John lives 3.4 miles from the grocery store. The bank is .6 miles farther than the store. How far does John live from the bank?

_____ _____ _____ = _____
number operation number   answer
        symbol

3. Tom bought .45 pounds of cheddar cheese and .39 pounds of swiss cheese. How much cheese did he buy in all?

_____ _____ _____ = _____
number operation number   answer
        symbol

6. Les has $14.35 more than Bill. Bill has $9.35. How much money does Less have?

_____ _____ _____ = _____
number operation number   answer
        symbol

Write a Question

When solving word problems, you must learn to read carefully. One way to learn this skill is to write your own questions.

1. Lauren spent $18.44. Dori spent $12.98.

    Write a question about the facts if the answer is:

    a) $31.42 _How much money_

    did they spend in all?

    _____

2. Shawna saved $45.50. Her sister saved $53.35.

    Write a question about the facts if the answer is:

    a) $98.85 _____

    _____

    _____

3. Ernesto spent $88.45 on groceries and $17.78 on gasoline.

    Write a question about the facts if the answer is:

    a) $106.23 _____

    _____

    _____

4. Tony bought 3 CDs for $12.99 each.

    Write a question about the facts if the answer is:

    a) $38.97 _____

    _____

    _____

5. Last month's telephone bill was $32.38. This month the bill is $88.45.

    Write a question about the facts if the answer is:

    a) $120.83 _____

    _____

    _____

6. John spent $5.50, Sal spent $6.75, and José spent 3.25.

    Write a question about the facts if the answer is:

    a) $15.50 _____

    _____

    _____

    b) $10.00 _____

    _____

    _____

Using Symbols

NUMBER RELATION SYMBOLS

$<$ is less than
$>$ is greater than
$=$ is equal to
$\neq$ is not equal to

Complete each statement with the correct symbol or amount.

1. Kia bought a television for $349.99. Jamal bought a television for $439.99.

   a) Jamal spent more than Kia.

   $439.99 _____ > _____ _____
   Jamal   symbol   Kia

   b) Kia spent less than Jamal.

   _____ _____ $439.99
   Kia   symbol   Jamal

   c) Kia and Jamal did not spend the same amount of money.

   _____ _____ _____
   Kia   symbol   Jamal

2. Jamie spent $35.59. Alia spent $44.54.

   a) How much did they spend altogether?

   $35.59 + _____ _____ _____
   Jamie   symbol   Alia   symbol   answer

   b) Jamie spent less than Alia.

   $35.59 _____ _____
   Jamie   symbol   Alia

   c) Alia spent more than Jamie.

   $44.54 _____ _____
   Alia   symbol   Jamie

   d) Jamie and Alia did not spend the same amount of money.

   _____ _____ _____
   Jamie   symbol   Alia

Two-Step Word Problems

Many situations require more than one step to get an answer.

A. Hector paid $3.79 for a burger and $1.25 for a shake. How much did he pay for both?

$3.79 + $1.25 = _____
Step 1

B. After he paid, he decided to buy french fries for $1.00. How much was his bill altogether

$5.04 + _____
Step 2

Solve each step below.

1. Gina and Hana spent the weekend making phone calls for a telemarketer. The number of calls each of them made is listed below.

	Saturday	Sunday
Gina	78	93
Hana	84	79

    a) How many calls did Gina make in all? _____

    b) How many calls did Hana make in all? _____

    c) Who made the most calls? _____

2. Dario and Lorena decided to find out who could run farther in one week. The distances they ran are listed below.

	Sunday	Monday	Tuesday	Wednesday	Thursday	Fridays	Saturday
Dario	3.4 mi	2.5 mi	5.5 mi		4.5 mi	3.0 mi	
Lorena		4.4 mi	6.0 mi	3.5 mi		5.0 mi	4.0 mi

    a) How far did Dario run? _____

    b) How far did Lorena run? _____

    c) Who ran farther? _____

    d) Use $<$, $>$, or $=$ to write a number sentence showing who ran farther.

    _____ _____ _____

number   symbol   number

Addition Word Problems

1. Pauline received checks for $34.99 and $29.00. How much money has she received?

_____ _____ _____ = _____
number operation number   answer
        symbol

2. Sachi bought a DVD player for $129.99 and three DVDs for $15.00 each. How much did she spend altogether?

_____ _____ _____ = _____
number operation number   answer
        symbol

3. Nathan's lunch bill was $14.35. He left a tip of $2.80. How much did lunch cost in total?

_____ _____ _____ = _____
number operation number   answer
        symbol

4. Bertha earned 49.5 points during the first round of the game and 55.6 points during the second round. What are her total points?

_____ _____ _____ = _____
number operation number   answer
        symbol

5. Kenya has $445.80 in her checking account. She was paid $129.89 this week. What is the balance in her checking account?

_____ _____ _____ = _____
number operation number   answer
        symbol

6. The car repairs cost $59.39 and gasoline cost $29.85. What is the total expense?

_____ _____ _____ = _____
number operation number   answer
        symbol

7. Benita saved $47.35 the first week, $59.75 the second week, and $88.67 the third week. How much has she saved?

Answer: _____

8. Bill's dentist bill was $137.50. He made payments of $45.50, $35.75, $20.50.

How much has he paid? _____

Does he need to pay more? _____

Addition Problem-Solving Review

Solve each problem.

1. Find the total.

Answer: _____

2.

$1.25 $3.55 $1.27

How much did José spend for lunch?

Answer: _____

3. Sandy bought 3 shirts for $18.99 each. She also bought 2 skirts for $24.99 each. How much did she spend in all?

Answer: _____

4. The odometer on Tony's car read 33,459.67 before he drove to Revelstoke. The trip to Revelstoke was 547.44 miles. What was the final odometer reading?

Answer: _____

5. Masami spent $4.58 on origami paper. She also bought rice paper for $5.98. If the tax was $1.03, what was her total?

Answer: _____

Steps for Subtraction

Step 1: Line up the decimal points and place values.

Step 2: Bring down the decimal point for the answer.

Step 3: Subtract the numbers.

$$.9 - .3 =$$

$$\begin{array}{r} .9 \\ -\ .3 \\ \hline .6 \end{array}$$

A. $7.3 - 3.1 =$

$$\begin{array}{r} 7.3 \\ -\ 3.1 \\ \hline \underline{}.\underline{} \end{array}$$
finish

B. $.38 - .04 =$

$$\begin{array}{r} .38 \\ -\ .04 \\ \hline .\underline{} \end{array}$$
finish

Line up the decimal points and place values. Subtract the numbers.

1. $.6 - .4 =$

2. $.9 - .5 =$

3. $.8 - .2 =$

4. $8.5 - 5.2 =$

5. $4.8 - 3.5 =$

6. $9.7 - 4.0 =$

7. $.16 - .05 =$

8. $.94 - .71 =$

9. $.78 - .57 =$

Regrouping

Step 1: Line up the decimal points and place values.

Step 2: Bring down the decimal point for the answer.

Step 3: Subtract the numbers. Regroup when necessary.

A. $.84 - .77 =$

$$
\begin{array}{r}
\overset{7\;14}{.\cancel{8}\cancel{4}} \\
- .77 \\
\hline
.\underline{} \\
\text{finish}
\end{array}
$$

B. $5.6 - 3.8 =$

$$
\begin{array}{r}
\overset{4\;\;16}{\cancel{5}.\cancel{6}} \\
- 3.8 \\
\hline
\underline{}.\underline{} \\
\text{finish}
\end{array}
$$

C. $4.83 - .91 =$

$$
\begin{array}{r}
\overset{3\;\;18}{\cancel{4}.\cancel{8}3} \\
- .91 \\
\hline
\underline{}.\underline{} \\
\text{finish}
\end{array}
$$

Subtract the numbers. Regroup when necessary.

1. $.31 - .23 =$

4. $8.3 - 2.5 =$

7. $8.57 - .82 =$

2. $.77 - .39 =$

5. $7.6 - 2.8 =$

8. $5.19 - 3.63 =$

3. $.41 - .18 =$

6. $4.4 - 2.7 =$

9. $6.76 - 1.94 =$

Mastering Regrouping

A. $.758 - .149 =$

$$
\begin{array}{r}
\overset{4}{}\overset{18}{} \\
.7\cancel{5}\cancel{8} \\
- .149 \\
\hline
.\underline{} \\
\text{finish}
\end{array}
$$

B. $.875 - .297 =$

$$
\begin{array}{r}
\overset{7}{}\overset{6}{}\overset{15}{} \\
.\cancel{8}\cancel{7}\cancel{5} \\
- .297 \\
\hline
.\underline{} \\
\text{finish}
\end{array}
$$

16 ⟵ regroup twice if necessary

C. 7.0

$$
\begin{array}{r}
\overset{6}{}\overset{9}{}\overset{\text{15}}{} \\
7.0\cancel{3} \\
- 3.67 \\
\hline
\underline{}.\underline{} \\
\text{finish}
\end{array}
$$

Subtract the numbers. Regroup when necessary.

1. $.693 - .405 =$

4. $.627 - .228 =$

7. $8.02 - 2.53 =$

2. $.973 - .615 =$

5. $.724 - .567 =$

8. $5.06 - 1.89 =$

3. $.075 - .046 =$

6. $.546 - .279 =$

9. $6.01 - 4.62 =$

More Regrouping

When you subtract decimals, you may need to fill in the empty place values with zeros. Adding zeros **after** the last digit of a decimal does not change the value:

$$.25 = .250$$

A. $3.7 - .31 =$

$$\begin{array}{r} \overset{6\ \ 10}{3.7\cancel{0}} \\ -\ \ .31 \\ \hline \underline{\ \ }.\underline{\ \ }\,\underline{\ \ } \end{array}$$ ← A zero must be added here.

finish

B. $5.9 - .62 =$

$$\begin{array}{r} \overset{8\ \ 10}{5.9\cancel{0}} \\ -\ \ .62 \\ \hline \underline{\ \ }.\underline{\ \ }\,\underline{\ \ } \end{array}$$

finish

C. $2.7 - .73 =$

$$\begin{array}{r} \overset{16}{} \\ \overset{1\ \ \cancel{6}\ 10}{2.7\cancel{0}} \\ -\ \ .73 \\ \hline \underline{\ \ }.\underline{\ \ }\,\underline{\ \ } \end{array}$$

finish

Subtract the numbers. Add zeros when necessary.

1. $4.7 - .36 =$

$$\begin{array}{r} \overset{6\ \ 10}{4.7\cancel{0}} \\ -\ \ .36 \\ \hline \underline{\ \ }.\underline{\ \ }\,\underline{\ \ } \end{array}$$

finish

4. $7.6 - .45 =$

7. $2.2 - .66 =$

2. $9.2 - .63 =$

5. $5.1 - .08 =$

8. $3.5 - .83 =$

3. $7.1 - .41 =$

6. $4.2 - .48 =$

9. $7.3 - .51 =$

Zeros Help

Adding zeros after the last digit of a decimal does not change the value.

.6 − .342 =

$$\begin{array}{r} \overset{5\ 9\ 10}{.\boxed{6\ 0\ 0}} \\ -\ .342 \\ \hline -\ .258 \end{array}$$

← Zeros must be added here.

Both decimal numbers **must** have the same number of decimal places.

Subtract the numbers. Add zeros to the decimal when necessary.

1. .8 − .316 =

$$\begin{array}{r} .800 \\ -.316 \\ \hline \end{array}$$

5. 9.3 − 2.207 =

9. .6 − .183 =

2. .6 − .137 =

6. .4 − .139 =

10. .4 − .205 =

3. 4.7 − .355 =

7. .8 − .504 =

11. .5 − .008 =

4. .5 − .438 =

8. 7.2 − .138 =

12. 5.7 − 1.063 =

Zeros at Work

A. $90.03 - 4.75 =$

B. $70.05 - 5.78 =$

C. $40.02 - 5.55 =$

$$
\begin{array}{r}
\overset{8}{}\overset{9}{}\overset{9}{}\overset{13}{} \\
\boxed{9\,0\,.\,0}\,3 \\
-\ \ 4\,.\,7\,5 \\
\hline
\underline{}.\underline{} \\
\text{finish}
\end{array}
$$

$$
\begin{array}{r}
\overset{6}{}\overset{9}{}\overset{9}{}\overset{15}{} \\
\boxed{7\,0\,.\,0}\,5 \\
-\ \ 5\,.\,7\,8 \\
\hline
\underline{}.\underline{} \\
\text{finish}
\end{array}
$$

$$
\begin{array}{r}
\overset{3}{}\overset{9}{}\overset{9}{}\overset{12}{} \\
\boxed{4\,0\,.\,0}\,2 \\
-\ \ 5\,.\,5\,5 \\
\hline
\underline{}.\underline{} \\
\text{finish}
\end{array}
$$

Subtract the numbers. Regroup when necessary.

1. $50.05 - 3.19 =$

4. $90.07 - 43.09 =$

7. $60.09 - 9.94 =$

2. $80.05 - 7.56 =$

5. $60.07 - 8.69 =$

8. $20.06 - 17.79 =$

3. $60.02 - 19.36 =$

6. $30.09 - 7.34 =$

9. $70.05 - 6.40 =$

Subtracting Decimals from Whole Numbers

When subtracting a decimal from a whole number, make sure you put the decimal point to the right of the whole number. Fill in the empty place values with zeros.

whole number

A. $8 - 1.5 =$

$$
\begin{array}{r}
^{7}\ ^{10} \\
\cancel{8}.\cancel{0} \\
- 1.5 \\
\hline
\_\_.\_\_
\end{array}
$$
finish

whole number

B. $5 - 3.82 =$

$$
\begin{array}{r}
^{4}\ ^{9}\ ^{10} \\
\boxed{\cancel{5}.\cancel{0}\cancel{0}} \\
- 3.82 \\
\hline
\_\_.\_\_\_
\end{array}
$$
finish

whole number

C. $7 - .063 =$

$$
\begin{array}{r}
^{6}\ ^{9}\ ^{9}\ ^{10} \\
\boxed{\cancel{7}.\cancel{0}\cancel{0}\cancel{0}} \\
- \ .063 \\
\hline
\_\_.\_\_\_\_
\end{array}
$$
finish

Subtract the numbers. Add zeros when necessary and regroup.

1. $6 - 4.1 =$

4. $7 - 4.43 =$

7. $3 - .018 =$

2. $10 - 3.5 =$

5. $22 - 4.06 =$

8. $9 - .713 =$

3. $20 - 5.7 =$

6. $18 - 3.82 =$

9. $5 - .024 =$

Subtracting Whole Numbers from Mixed Decimals

Use zeros to hold empty place values when you subtract whole numbers from decimals.

A.
whole number

$34.5 - 9 =$

$$
\begin{array}{r}
{\scriptstyle 2\ 14} \\
\cancel{3}\cancel{4}.5 \\
-\ \ \ 9.0 \longleftarrow \text{ fill in zero} \\
\hline
\underline{\ \ \ }\ .\underline{\ \ } \\
\text{finish}
\end{array}
$$

B.
whole number

$46.43 - 17 =$

$$
\begin{array}{r}
{\scriptstyle 3\ 16} \\
\cancel{4}\cancel{6}.43 \\
-17.00 \\
\hline
\underline{\ \ \ }\ .\underline{\ \ \ } \\
\text{finish}
\end{array}
$$

C.
whole number

$87.849 - 35 =$

$$
\begin{array}{r}
87.849 \\
-\ 35.000 \\
\hline
\underline{\ \ \ }\ .\underline{\ \ \ \ } \\
\text{finish}
\end{array}
$$

Write in zeros when needed. Line up the decimal points and the numbers. Subtract.

1. $27.8 - 18 =$

2. $86.1 - 40 =$

3. $50.3 - 13 =$

4. $45.19 - 8 =$

5. $186.70 - 21 =$

6. $17.62 - 9 =$

7. $52.691 - 45 =$

8. $41.512 - 23 =$

9. $75.822 - 18 =$

Watch Out for Whole Numbers

whole number

A. $6 - .14 =$

$$\begin{array}{r} ^{5}^{9}^{10} \\ 6.00 \\ - .14 \\ \hline \underline{}.\underline{} \\ \text{finish} \end{array}$$

whole number

B. $72.2 - 5 =$

$$\begin{array}{r} ^{6}^{12} \\ 72.2 \\ - 5.0 \\ \hline \underline{}.\underline{} \\ \text{finish} \end{array}$$

C. $35.5 - 8.9 =$

$$\begin{array}{r} 35.5 \\ - 8.9 \\ \hline \underline{}.\underline{} \\ \text{finish} \end{array}$$

Line up the decimal points and the numbers. Write zeros when necessary. Subtract.

1. $8 - .76 =$

4. $27.65 - 3 =$

7. $68.89 - 59.19 =$

2. $71.1 - 7.3 =$

5. $21.2 - 7.5 =$

8. $96.4 - 3 =$

3. $20 - 15.78 =$

6. $92.5 - 23 =$

9. $7 - .92 =$

Add or Subtract?

Do the following addition and subtraction problems carefully.

1. $5.8 + 3.6 =$

2. $71.5 - 19.6 =$

3. $194.45 - 76.98 =$

4. $87.44 - 48.58 =$

5. $2.93 + 5.6 =$

6. $.84 + 2.9 + 8 =$

7. $71.5 - 25.37 =$

8. $30.09 - 9.15 =$

9. $34.6 - 7.43 =$

10. $9 + 45.9 =$

11. $.94 + .07 =$

12. $732.37 - 21.7 =$

Putting It All Together

Place the symbols <, >, or = in the ◯ to make each true.

1. 5.6 + 8.9 ◯ 21 − 6.4

    14.5   14.6

2. 3.65 + 4.17 ◯ 14.85 − 7.25

3. 90.03 − 57.3 ◯ 28.5 + 4.7

4. 4.62 + 8.05 + 54.73 ◯ 79.4 − 12.67

5. 62.9 − 15 ◯ 42.5 + 5.105

6. 21.4 + 9 ◯ 15.8 + 14.6

7. 267.75 − 125.24 ◯ 65.89 + 78.99

8. .82 + .47 ◯ 6.84 − 5.55

Subtraction Review

Practice your subtraction skills.

1. $.78 - .54 =$

2. $6.7 - 4.3 =$

3. $.45 - .37 =$

4. $5.75 - 4.56 =$

5. $.328 - .269 =$

6. $.6 - .19 =$

7. $3.4 - 2.25 =$

8. $.8 - .242 =$

9. $1.2 - .67 =$

10. $27 - .725 =$

11. $55.34 - 26 =$

12. Which of the following is less than 7.12?

   7.5   16   .633

Number Sentences

1. Read over the facts several times to make sure you understand them.

2. Think about the facts in the problem and what you are being asked to find.

3. Complete the number sentence for each problem.

4. Ask yourself, "Does the answer make sense?"

Complete each number sentence.

1. Anne's favorite candy bar used to weigh 2.4 ounces. Its size was changed, and it now weighs .21 ounces less. How many ounces does the new size weigh?

_____	_____	_____	=	_____
number	operation symbol	number		answer

5. Andrea's car has a 15.8 gallon gas tank. If she has 2.9 gallons in the tank, how many gallons are needed to fill up the tank?

_____	_____	_____	=	_____
number	operation symbol	number		answer

2. Karen drove 118.6 miles the first day and 69.8 miles the second day. How many miles did she drive in all?

_____	_____	_____	=	_____
number	operation symbol	number		answer

6. Tina bought 1.53 pounds of trail mix and .75 pounds of chocolate-covered raisins. How much did she buy in all?

_____	_____	_____	=	_____
number	operation symbol	number		answer

3. A fishing rod costs $32.45. Dave has saved $9.50. How much more does Dave need to buy the fishing rod?

_____	_____	_____	=	_____
number	operation symbol	number		answer

7. A new radio costs $75.95. Kyle has $22.75. How much more will Kyle need to buy the radio?

_____	_____	_____	=	_____
number	operation symbol	number		answer

4. Randy saved $38.90 and his sister saved $4.50. How much more money did Randy save than his sister?

_____	_____	_____	=	_____
number	operation symbol	number		answer

8. Mr. Bellson saved $125.00. Mr. Martinez saved $95.00. How much more money did Mr. Bellson save than Mr. Martinez?

_____	_____	_____	=	_____
number	operation symbol	number		answer

Does the Answer Make Sense?

Write number sentences for each problem below. Then write the answer in the sentence below the problem. Read it and ask yourself, "Does the answer make sense?"

1. Alice has a temperature of 101.4.° A normal temperature is 98.6.° How many degrees above normal is Alice's temperature?

_____ _____ _____ = _____
number operation number   answer
        symbol

Alice's temperature is _____° above normal.

2. Henry drove 172.8 miles before his car broke down. He had 39.6 miles left to travel. How many miles did he want to travel in all?

_____ _____ _____ = _____
number operation number   answer
        symbol

Henry wanted to travel _____ miles.

3. A storm door cost $99.95. Wes paid with a $25.00 discount coupon. How much did he pay for the storm door?

_____ _____ _____ = _____
number operation number   answer
        symbol

Wes paid $_____ for the storm door.

4. The dinner costs $14.35. How much change will you get back from $20.00?

_____ _____ _____ = _____
number operation number   answer
        symbol

You will get $_____ back in change.

5. Mr. Smith paid $1,258.15 in taxes this year. Last year he paid $1,217.92. How much more did he pay in taxes this year?

_____ _____ _____ = _____
number operation number   answer
        symbol

Mr. Smith paid $_____ more in taxes this year.

6. Adam rode his bike 31.4 miles on Monday and 44.3 miles on Tuesday. How many miles did he ride in two days?

_____ _____ _____ = _____
number operation number   answer
        symbol

Adam rode _____ miles in two days.

Using Symbols

NUMBER RELATION SYMBOLS
< is less than
> is greater than
= is equal to
≠ is not equal to

Complete each statement with the correct symbol or amount.

1. Alice spent $14.89. Ellen spent $9.40. How much more money did Alice spend than Ellen?

   a) Alice spent $5.49 more than Ellen. $9.40 + _____ = $14.89
   Ellen   answer   Alice

   b) Ellen spent $5.49 less than Alice. $14.89 – _____ = $9.40
   Alice   answer   Ellen

   c) Alice spent a greater amount of money than Ellen.
   _____ > _____
   Alice   Ellen

   d) Ellen spent a lesser amount of money than Alice.
   _____ < _____
   Ellen   Alice

   e) Alice and Ellen did not spend the same amount of money.
   $14.89 _____ $9.40
   Alice   symbol   Ellen

2. Sue spent $45.33. Janet spent $17.19. How much more money did Sue spend than Janet?

   a) Sue spent $28.14 more than Janet. $17.19 + _____ = $45.33
   Janet   answer   Sue

   b) Janet spent $28.14 less than Sue. $45.33 – _____ = $17.19
   Sue   answer   Janet

   c) Sue spent a greater amount of money than Janet.
   _____ > _____
   Sue   Janet

   d) Janet spent a lesser amount of money than Sue.
   _____ < _____
   Janet   Sue

   e) Sue and Janet did not spend the same amount of money.
   $45.33 _____ $17.19
   Sue   symbol   Janet

Write a Question

To decide whether to add or subtract, you must read carefully. One way to learn to read carefully is to write your own question.

1. Leslie spent $15.35.
   Dawn spent $9.98.

   Write a question about the facts if the answer is:

   a) $25.33 _How much money_
   did they spend in all? ___

   b) $5.37 _____
   _____

2. Sean saved $52.29, and his sister saved $9.13.

   Write a question about the facts if the answer is:

   a) $43.16 _____
   _____

   b) $61.42 _____
   _____

3. Erica's groceries cost $14.75, and her gasoline cost $8.68.

   Write a question about the facts if the answer is:

   a) $23.43 _____
   _____

   b) $6.07 _____
   _____

4. Tina bought a jacket for $84.65 and a sweater for $20.95.

   Write a question about the facts if the answer is:

   a) $63.70 _____
   _____

   b) $105.60 _____
   _____

5. Mr. Alatalo saved $135.00.
   Mr. Forbes saved $45.50.

   Write a question about the facts if the answer is:

   a) $180.50 _____
   _____

   b) $89.50 _____
   _____

6. This year Mr. Fenwick paid $238.16 in taxes. Last year he paid $198.30.

   Write a question about the facts if the answer is:

   a) $436.46 _____
   _____

   b) $39.86 _____
   _____

Decide to Add or Subtract

1. Read the facts carefully.
2. Decide whether to write an addition or subtraction question.
3. Write a question and a number sentence.
4. Check your answer with the question. Ask yourself, "Does the answer make sense?"

Write a question for **either an addition problem or a subtraction problem.**
Then complete a number sentence.

1. Pete had $15.00. He spent $7.95.

   a) Question __How much money__
   __did he have left?__

   b) _____ _____ _____ = _____
   number   operation   number   answer
            symbol

2. Last week Janie earned $45.65. This week she earned $29.98.

   a) Question _____

   _____

   b) _____ _____ _____ = _____
   number   operation   number   answer
            symbol

3. A new radio costs $83.45. Jack has $33.45.

   a) Question _____

   _____

   b) _____ _____ _____ = _____
   number   operation   number   answer
            symbol

4. Bill added $25.75 to his savings of $400.95.

   a) Question _____

   _____

   b) _____ _____ _____ = _____
   number   operation   number   answer
            symbol

5. Al had $20.00. Dinner cost $13.49.

   a) Question _____

   _____

   b) _____ _____ _____ = _____
   number   operation   number   answer
            symbol

6. Barbara has $15.19 more than Lana. Lana has $7.83.

   a) Question _____

   _____

   b) _____ _____ _____ = _____
   number   operation   number   answer
            symbol

Mixed Addition and Subtraction

Decide whether to add or subtract. Write the answer in the statement below. Ask yourself, "Does this answer make sense?"

1. Mary bought a suit for $165.34 and a blouse for $34.95. How much did she pay altogether?

_____ + _____ = _____
number   operation   number   answer
           symbol

Mary paid $_____ altogether.

2. How much change would you receive from $5.00 if your bill was $2.91?

_____ _____ _____ = _____
number   operation   number   answer
           symbol

You would receive $_____ in change.

3. Dominic drove 256.3 miles on Monday and 136.9 miles on Tuesday. How many total miles did he drive?

_____ _____ _____ = _____
number   operation   number   answer
           symbol

Dominic drove _____ total miles.

4. Gert bought 5.4 pounds of ground beef last week and 3.2 pounds this week. She bought how many pounds of ground beef altogether?

_____ _____ _____ = _____
number   operation   number   answer
           symbol

Gert bought _____ pounds for both weeks.

5. If the regular price is $45.32 and the sale price $36.50, how much can be saved by buying at the sale price?

_____ _____ _____ = _____
number   operation   number   answer
           symbol

$_____ can be saved by buying at the sale price.

6. Lucas bought a ticket to the game for $7.25. How much change will he receive from $10.00?

_____ _____ _____ = _____
number   operation   number   answer
           symbol

Lucas will receive $_____ in change.

7. The grocery bill amounted to $29.15. Gasoline for the car came to $18.11. What was the cost of both items?

_____ _____ _____ = _____
number   operation   number   answer
           symbol

The cost of both items is $_____.

8. The bus fare is $12.25. How much change will you get back from $20.00?

_____ _____ _____ = _____
number   operation   number   answer
           symbol

You will get $_____ back in change.

Two-Step Word Problems

Many situations require more than one step to get an answer.

A. Shannon paid $2.79 for a sandwich and $1.35 for a malt. How much did she pay for both?

B. How much change will she get back from $20.00?

$2.79 + $1.35 = _____ $\boxed{+}$
Step 1

$20.00 - _____ $\boxed{-}$
Step 2

Do both steps below. Indicate the operation with $\boxed{+}$ or $\boxed{-}$.

1. a) Jody bought a camera for $79.95 and a calculator for $16.99. What did she pay for the camera and calculator? _____ $\boxed{}$

b) How much change will Jody get back from $100.00? _____ $\boxed{}$

2. a) At dinner, Joe got $4.00 change back from a $20 bill. How much did dinner cost? _____ $\boxed{}$

b) Joe left a $2.50 tip. How much did he spend altogether? _____ $\boxed{}$

3. a) Les walked 4.5 miles on Monday and 7.75 miles on Tuesday. How many miles did he walk? _____ $\boxed{}$

b) On the same two days last week he walked 15 miles. How much farther did he walk last week? _____ $\boxed{}$

4. a) Roger paid bills for $34 and $27.50. How much were his bills? _____ $\boxed{}$

b) He had to pay a late fee of $2.50 on the second bill. What was his total bill payment? _____ $\boxed{}$

5. a) Korene had $50.00. She spent $35.60 on groceries and $12.38 on gas. How much did she pay for the groceries and gas? _____ $\boxed{}$

b) How much does she have left from the $50.00? _____ $\boxed{}$

6. a) Gregory has $195.62 in his checking account. He wrote checks for $25.63 and $15.98. What was the total amount of the 2 checks? _____ $\boxed{}$

b) How much does Gregory have left in his checking account? _____ $\boxed{}$

Two-Step Problem Solving

When you recognize a two-step problem, write two questions.

This week Mr. Lasko spent $28.75 for food and $18.45 for gasoline. By how much did he go over his $45 budget?

Write Question 1: <u>How much did he spend in all?</u>
<u>$28.75 + $18.45 = $47.20</u>

Write Question 2: <u>By how much did he go over his budget?</u>
<u>$47.20 − $45.00 = $2.20</u>

Write two questions and solve the problems.

1. Danielle left for the ballgame with $25.00. She loaned her friend $8.50 and spent $12.95. How much did she have left?

   a) Question 1: _____

      _____

      _____

   b) Question 2: _____

      _____

      _____

2. Lin bought a necklace that cost $15.95 and two rings at $47.99 each. How much did she spend?

   a) Question 1: _____

      _____

   b) Question 2: _____

      _____

3. Lisa has $436.65 in her savings account. She deposits checks of $84.50, $196.38, and $36.47. After making the deposit, how much will Lisa have in her savings?

   a) Question 1: _____

      _____

      _____

   b) Question 2: _____

      _____

      _____

4. Heidi's grocery bill without coupons came to $45.25. She has coupons of $.35, $.15, $.25, $.65, and $.09. How much will Heidi pay for groceries with the coupons?

   a) Question 1: _____

      _____

      _____

   b) Question 2: _____

      _____

      _____

Multistep Word Problems

To solve problems with many steps, write several questions.

Calvin's dinner bill came to $28.35 plus $1.42 tax.
He paid for his dinner with 2 twenty-dollar bills.
What was his change?

Question 1: What was his bill?	$28.35 + $1.42 = $29.77
Question 2: How much did he pay?	2 × $20 = $ 40
Question 3: What was his change?	$40 − $29.77 = $10.23

Write questions and solve the problems on another sheet of paper.

1. Muriel bought four items at the hardware store which cost $2.15, $.98, $1.54, and $3.05. The sales tax amounted to $.39. How much change did she receive from 2 five-dollar bills?

   Question 1: _____

   Question 2: _____

   Question 3: _____

2. The Nuyen family had their annual dental checkup. Mr. Nuyen's bill was $98.00. His wife's bill was $54.75, and their two sons' were $35.00 each. If dental insurance paid $123.14, how much did the family have to pay?

   Question 1: _____

   Question 2: _____

   Question 3: _____

3. Chris entered a 25-mile bicycle race. She traveled 10.4 miles the first hour. During the second hour, she traveled 1.4 miles less than the first hour. How many more miles did she have to go?

   Question 1: _____

   Question 2: _____

   Question 3: _____

4. Millie's checking account had $98.26 in it.
   Week 1: wrote check for $20.56
   Week 2: made deposit of $75.00
   Week 3: wrote check for $15.79
   How much did she have in her account at the end of the third week?

   Question 1: _____

   Question 2: _____

   Question 3: _____

Picture Problems

Amount Given Clerk	Amount Spent	Amount of Change Received
$15.00	$13.37	$
$30.00	$25.67	$
$20.00	$17.08	$

Cost of First Mile	Cost of Second Mile	Cost of Additional Mile
$2.60	$1.20	$.95

4. What is the total amount of change received? _____

1. If Olga traveled 3 miles by taxi, how much change will she receive from 2 five-dollar bills?

_____

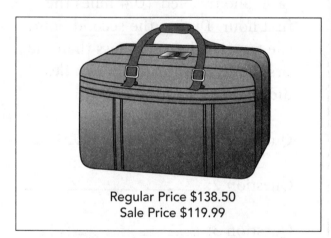

Regular Price $138.50
Sale Price $119.99

BROOM
$19.08

PAINT

ONE GALLON

PAINT
$18.32

5. If you decided to buy both items, how much would you get back from two twenty-dollar bills?

_____

2. How much less is the sale price?

_____

Regular Price $68.98
Sale Price $52.48

WEEKLY SAVINGS	
Week	Savings
1	$24.50
2	15.95
3	30.75
4	32.05

3. How much is saved by buying the sleeping bag on sale? _____

6. Leon wants to save two hundred dollars. How much more must he save? _____

Subtraction Problem-Solving Review

Solve each problem.

1. Christopher used to weigh 127.55 pounds. Now he weighs 135.43 pounds. How much weight did he gain?

    Answer: _____

2. Jackie bought 3.45 pounds of fish and ate 2.25 pounds. How much did she have left?

    Answer: _____

3. Jorge's temperature was 103.4° on Monday. By Tuesday it had dropped to 99.3°. By how much did his temperature drop?

    Answer: _____

4. A monthly bus pass costs $45.00. Gasoline and tolls cost $55.75. How much is saved by taking the bus?

    Answer: _____

5. The restaurant bill came to $57.33. How much change will Donna receive if she gives the waiter $60.00?

    Answer: _____

6. Lenora bought three movie tickets for $8.75 each and popcorn for $4.00. How much will she get back if she pays with $50?

    Answer: _____

7. Anne had $765.50 in her checking account. She wrote a check for $44.98. Then she deposited $60.70. What is her new balance?

    Answer: _____

8. Danny wrote the following checks: $112.34, $132.32, $144.58. If his starting balance was $485.98, what is the new balance?

    Answer: _____

Reading Temperatures

Thermometers use decimal places to show temperature.

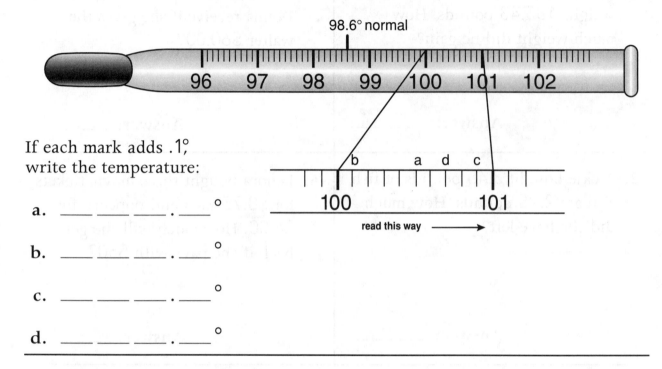

If each mark adds .1°,
write the temperature:

a. ___ ___ ___ . ___ °

b. ___ ___ ___ . ___ °

c. ___ ___ ___ . ___ °

d. ___ ___ ___ . ___ °

1. What is normal temperature? _____
    Put an ↓ above it on the thermometer.

2. Jane's son had a temperature 1.5° above normal.
    What was his temperature? _____
    Put a ○ above it on the thermometer.

3. In an hour, his temperature was 102.3°.
    How many more degrees did it rise in that hour? _____
    Put a ☐ above 102.3° on the thermometer.

4. Jane treated her son's fever and called the doctor to report
    that the fever had dropped to normal.
    How many degrees did it drop? _____

Decimals: Addition & Subtraction

Figuring Change

CLEANING BILL		
TOTAL:	$15.50	

pay this bill

use $20.00

A. $ ____ . ____

− ____ . ____

$ __ . __
find change

Find the amount of change left from each bill.

1.

EAT AT JOE'S	
Burger	3.50
Fries	1.25
Coke	.95
Tax	.50
Total	$6.20

pay for lunch

use $10.00

$ ____ . ____

− ____ . ____

$ __ . __

2.

ELECTRIC BILL
$23.49

pay bill

use this

$

−
_____

3.

SUE'S SHOP	
2 skirts	$40.00
Tax	3.50
Total	$43.50

pay for purchase

use this

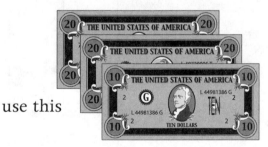

$

−
_____

4.

$1.75 each

use this

$

−
_____

Making Change

Find the amount of change and its money form. Use the least number of bills and coins possible.

Cost: $5.95　　$10.00
Paid: $10.00　− $ 5.95
　　　　　　　　$ 4.05

1. Cost: $12.92　＿＿.＿＿
   Paid: $20.00　−＿＿.＿＿

2. Cost: $3.48　　＿.＿＿
   Paid: $5.00　　−＿.＿＿

3. Cost: $14.83
   Paid: $15.00

4. Cost: $.84
   Paid: $5.00

5. Cost: $2.41
   Paid: $10.00

	$5	$1	25¢	10¢	5¢	1¢
		4			1	
1.						
2.						
3.						
4.						
5.						

Money Problems

Regular Price $12.78
Sale Price $9.08

$54.98 $10.29

$60.49 $5.69

1. If Mr. Harper buys the flashlight at the sale price, how much change will he get back from a ten-dollar bill?

_____

2.

ITEM	PRICE
Bicycle	$179.85
Lock	5.75
Headlights	13.59
Speedometer	37.99
Subtotal	
Sales Tax	14.23
Total Cost	

What is the total cost of the 4 items?

_____

3. Jerry paid for the new watch with a 50-dollar bill. He received $3.65 in change. How much did the watch cost? _____

4. a) Which would cost less, the jacket and the clock or the camera and the flashlight? _____

   b) How much less? _____

Sandwich
$3.84

French Fries
$.87

Cola
$.93

Onion Rings
$1.25

5. What 3 items did Brian buy for lunch if he got exactly $4.36 back from ten dollars?

   a) _____

   b) _____

   c) _____

Keeping Records

On a fishing trip, Mr. Gonzalez and his son weighed their four largest fish. The results are listed in the chart.

Fish	Weight
1	2.39 pounds
2	3.23 pounds
3	3.5 pounds
4	6.01 pounds

1. What is the combined weight of the four fish? _____

2. Arrange the weights of the fish from largest to smallest.

   _____ _____ _____ _____

       largest   smallest

3. What is the difference in weight between the largest and the smallest fish?

   _____

4. Mr. Gonzalez's son caught the 2 largest fish. How much more did these weigh than the 2 smallest? _____

5. Mr. Gonzalez's expenses for the fishing trip are listed below:
   Meals $48.70
   Bait 8.25
   Gas 43.13
   Lodging 85.98
   Boat Rental 50.00

   If Mr. Gonzalez budgeted $250 for the trip, by how many dollars was he under his budget? _____

6. From the expense figures, which three items total exactly $142.93?

   a) _____ b) _____ c) _____

Breaking the Record

Maria, Shara, Carrie, and Nancy are on the girls' 400-meter relay team. Their individual times at the meet were:

Maria	12.58 seconds	Carrie	13.86 seconds
Shara	13.2 seconds	Nancy	12.4 seconds

1. What is the total time for the relay team? _____ seconds

2. If the school record is 51.6 seconds, the team must run _____ seconds faster to tie the school record.

3. List the girls' names and times from fastest to slowest.

   a) _____   _____ fastest

   b) _____   _____

   c) _____   _____

   d) _____   _____ slowest

4. What is the difference between the fastest and slowest times?

   _____ seconds

5. At the next meet, the 400-meter relay team members ran their best time of 51.48 seconds. Did they break the school record? _____ If so, by how many seconds? _____

Life-Skills Math Review

Solve each of the following problems.

1. In the morning Jane's son had a temperature of 103.2. By dinner it had dropped to 99.4. How many degrees did the temperature drop?

   Answer: _____

2. Joel's taxi bill was $18.50. How much change would he receive from $20?

   Answer: _____

3. Pia bought some groceries for $12.43. She paid with a 20-dollar bill. How much of each bill and coin did she receive as change? Use the least number of bills and coins.

   _____ 1-dollar   _____ 5-dollar   _____ quarter

   _____ dime   _____ nickel   _____ penny

4. The local sport store had a sale. Betty bought the following items: basketball $22.95, soccer jersey $30.55, running shoes $45.25. If the sales tax was $7.92, how much was her total cost?

   Answer: _____

5. Pamela ran 7.5 miles on Sunday, 4.3 miles on Tuesday, 5.6 miles on Wednesday, and 4.6 miles on Friday. How far did she run during the week?

   Answer: _____

Addition and Subtraction Review

1. Use <, >, or = to complete the number sentence.

   a) .400 _____ .40

   b) .5 _____ .49

2. Write the decimals in order from least to greatest.

   10.06   10.6   10.64

   _____ _____ _____
   least   greatest

3. 5.69 + .033 + 14 =

   Answer: _____

4. 4.556 + 8.02 + 4 =

   Answer: _____

5. Combine $13.85 and $9.98.

   Answer: _____

6. .94 − .83 =

   Answer: _____

7. .627 − .549 =

   Answer: _____

8. .9 − .357 =

   Answer: _____

9. Use <, >, or = to complete the number sentence.

   .84 + .49 ◯ 2.45 − .76

10. Dinner cost $35.43. How much change would Dana receive if he paid with $50?

    Answer: _____

1. $57.41 + 8.6 =$

   Answer: _____

2. Alison bought a hamburger and a soft drink for $3.43. How much change did she get back from $20.00?

   Answer: _____

3. $4.07 - 2.58 =$

   Answer: _____

4. In the number 10.386, which digit is in the hundredths place?

   Answer: _____

5. $3.51 + 8 + 13.65 =$

   Answer: _____

6. Nathan added $69.63 to his savings of $149.35. How much does he have in his savings altogether?

   Answer: _____

7. $75 - 23.15 =$

   Answer: _____

8. Write twelve and seventeen thousandths with numbers.

   Answer: _____

9. Reggie had $5.00. He spent $2.38. How much money does he have left?

   Answer: _____

10. $13 - 9.46 =$

   Answer: _____

11. $8.9 + 2.407 =$

Answer: _____

12. Rita bought a suit for $83.19 and a blouse for $27.95. How much did she pay altogether?

Answer: _____

13.
$$\begin{array}{r} 7.72 \\ -2.57 \\ \hline \end{array}$$

Answer: _____

14. From a board 2.75 meters long, Steve cut a smaller board 1.8 meters long. How long was the remaining board?

Answer: _____

15. Which of the following is equal to 7.3: .73, 7.03, 7.300, or 7.030?

Answer: _____

16. Find the combined weight of three packages that weigh 2.2 pounds, 1.9 pounds, and 4.15 pounds.

Answer: _____

17. Arrange these numbers in order from least to greatest: 5.2, 5.09, 5.21.

_____ _____ _____
least   greatest

18. The distance from Maria's house to her son's school is 4.4 miles. From the school to Maria's job is another 7.7 miles. What is the distance from her house to her work by way of the school?

Answer: _____

19.
$$\begin{array}{r} 13.76 \\ .29 \\ 63.83 \\ + 5.41 \\ \hline \end{array}$$

Answer: _____

20. The normal rainfall for Chicago in August is 4.2 inches. One dry summer Chicago had only 1.9 inches of rain. How much below normal was the rainfall that summer?

Answer: _____

Evaluation Chart

On the following chart, circle the number of any problem you missed. The column after the problem number tells you the pages where those problems are taught. You should review the sections for any problems you missed.

Skill Area	Posttest Problem Number	Skill Section	Review Page
Place Value	4, 8, 15, 17	7–24	25
Addition	1, 5, 11, 19	26–34	35
Subtraction	3, 7, 10, 13	45–55	56
Addition Word Problems	6, 12, 16, 18	36–43	44
Subtraction Word Problems	2, 9, 14, 20	57–66	67
Life-Skills Math	All	68–73	74

bring down   to move the decimal point to the answer line
> 5.5 + 4.3 = 9.8
> ↑

budget   a plan for spending money
> I wrote a budget so I could save money.

checking account   a bank account used to pay bills
> I pay my bills with checks from my checking account.

circle   to draw a line around something
> Circle the correct answer:
>
> 2 + 4 =   4   ⑥   8

combined earnings   total earnings of more than one income
> My combined earnings from my two jobs is $425.00 per week.

coupons   a printed form or advertisement that can be used to reduce the price of an item
> I use the coupons from the Sunday paper to save money.

deposit   money put in a bank, or to put money in a bank
> I deposit money in my savings account every week.

digit   one of the ten number symbols: 0, 1, 2, 3, 4, 5, 6, 7, 8, and 9

discount coupon   a printed form or advertisement that can be used to reduce the price of an item
> The 20%-off discount coupon is only good this weekend.

expanded form   to write a math problem in the longest version
> 84 = 80 + 4

increased   to get larger or expand
> What is 5 increased by 3?
> 5 + 3 = 8

late fee   the money someone pays for returning something past the due date
> I had to pay a late fee when I returned my library book after it was due.

line up   to make sure the decimal points are in a line
>   4.4
>   5.6
> + 23.0
> ————
>   ↑

mixed decimal   the combination of a whole number and a decimal
> $2.45 is a mixed decimal

number relation symbol   symbols that explain two numbers

For example:

less than	<
greater than	>
equal to	=
not equal to	≠

15 is greater than 9

OR

15 > 9

operation symbol   the symbol (+, −, ×, ÷, =) that tells you what to do with a math problem

16 + 4 = 20
↑

place value   the name given to the space where a number is written

$12.75
↑

The 2 is in the ones place.

placeholder   a number (usually 0) that keeps a place in a problem and does not change the value of the number

$$0.233 \leftarrow$$
$$+ \ 8.000$$
$$\overline{8.233}$$

regroup (borrow)   to shift numbers to a lower place value

$$\overset{2\ 12}{\cancel{32}}$$
$$- \ \ \ 8$$
$$\overline{24}$$

regroup (carry)   to shift numbers to a higher place value

$$\overset{1}{18}$$
$$+ \ 4$$
$$\overline{22}$$

regular price   the cost of an item not on sale

I paid regular price because the shirt was not on sale.

sale price   the reduced cost of an item

The sale price of the shirt is very low.

savings account   a bank account used to save money

I put money in my savings account every week.

tax   money paid to the government

You bought a shirt for $18.00 plus $1.35 tax. What change will you get back if you paid with a $20 bill?

$$18.00$$
$$+ \ \ 1.35$$
$$\overline{19.35}$$

$$20.00$$
$$- \ 19.35$$
$$\overline{.65}$$

tip   money left for a waiter or waitress

My lunch cost $6.25 and I left a $1.00 tip.